Short and Sweet

100-Word Stories

by Pat Blosse

DiaBlo Publishing

Published by DiaBlo Publishing, 2024

ISBN: 9798884953314

First edition

Printed by Kindle Direct Publishing in the United Kingdom

Other books by Pat Blosse:

<u>Novels</u>

The Red Bonnet (a supernatural mystery thriller)

<u>Plays</u>

Heaven's Above (one-act play for children)

There Will be Some Slight Interference (one-act comedy)

In collaboration with Dennis Diamond

   The Cat Flap (three-act Agatha Christie spoof)

   The Ghosts of Martha Rudd (three-act ghostly comedy)

   Lost But Not Least (one-act Shakespearean drama)

   Sketches in Hyde Park (5-part radio play)

Contact:

patblosse@gmail.com or

on Facebook at Patrick Blosse_Author Page

Short and Sweet

100-Word Stories

by Pat Blosse

Copyright © 2024 Patrick Blosse.

All rights reserved

The characters and events portrayed in these stories are (mostly) fictitious. Any similarity to real persons, living or dead, is coincidental and not intended by the author, unless they are about the author, in which case he will deny everything.

No part of this book may be reproduced, or stored in a retrieval system, or transmitted in any form or by any means, electronic, mechanical, photocopying, recording, or otherwise, without express written permission of the publisher.

This page is blank for aesthetic purposes, or for doodling in.

Contents

Introduction 9

Love is a Many Splendored Thing 10

Handing Over	11
Duologue	12
Grannie Likes to Google	14
The Train Now Departing	15
Special Delivery	16
Valentine's Day Card	17
Tentative Steps	18
Virginal Valentine's Virtual Vicissitudes	
Part 1 – Reflection	19
Part 2 – Stormy Relationships	20

Families – Who'd 'ave 'em 22

The Jigsaw Murders	23
Grey Tunkle Bill	24
Taking the Micky	25
The Pies That Came in From the Cold	26
Dessert Island Dicks	27
Will This Lunacy Never End?	28
Let's Twist Again Like We Did Last Christmas	29
Moving Experience	30
How the Other Half Loves	31
The Thin End of the Edge Pieces	32
Sweet Justice	33

A Matter of Life and Death 35

What Are We Here For?	36
Look Who It Is!	37
Nurture v. Nature	38

Hungry for the Sea	39
Life	40
Just Chillin'	41
From Little Acorns	42
April	43
Friendly Fire	44

It's Not All 9 to 5..........46

Had a Good Day at School, Darling?	47
The Archer	48
Dress Down Day	49
The Stargazers	50
A Frosty Receptionist	51
Give Us a Break	52
The Rise and Fall of the Blue Whale	53
Life's a Beach	54
Morning Gloria	55

Near and Far..........57

Holiday Romances, Essex Style	58
Brief Encounters	59
Mildred	60
The Godfather of all Journeys	61
Talking Types Let Us Down Again	62
Dangerous Cornering by J B Priestlike	63
Downstage With Feeling	64
Sláinte – Good Health!	65

Never Work with Children and Animals..67

Angling for Success	68
Pronoun'cing Their Names	69
Chiumbo's First Christmas, 1899	70
Alice's Lost Adventure	71

Animal Instincts	72
Dear Santa	73
Hoomins is Weird	74
The Pragmatist's Fairy Tales by the Grim Buggers	75
What Goes Up Must Come Down	76

Ineptitude and Politics............................78

Humboldt	79
Cabinet Reshuffle	80
A Position of Trust	81
Order! Order!	82
The Green Room at the BBC	83
Boris in Blunderland	84
One to Bind Them All	85
Stealing Resolve	85
To Speak or Not to Speak, That is the Question	86
An Inspector Falls by J B Priestlike	87

Science or Fiction?............................89

A Hole in One's Theory	90
Infinity	91
Flapdoodle	92
Plumbing the Depths	93
Archie Mead's Principle	94
The Little Prick	95
Here We Go Again	96
Microcosmic Musings	97
The Dawn of a New Age	98
Dear Self	99
It's Only Natural	100

Time and Time Again	101

The Mystical and the Magical............103

A Magic Cure?	104
Unwanted Visitors	105
Lady Felicity Small	106
It's All Done With Smoke and Mirrors	107
Seven	108

Crime and Punishment........................110

Fall From Grace	111
Sins of the Father	112
The Best Laid Schemes	113
This Little Piggy	114
The Gumshoe	115
Inviting Displeasure	116
Claude the Burglar	117
Puffed Out	118
Knuckles Malone	119

Reeling and Writhing............................121

Lost for Words	122
Lost for More Words	122
The Townspeople Murder Mystery	123
No Rhyme or Reason	124
Warning! Colourful Language	125
Writing After Midnight	126
The Seat of Learning	127
Making His Mark	128
Piss-monunciation Syndrome	129
This Week's Latest Blockbuster	130
Nobody Likes Me, Everybody Hates Me, I'm Going Down the Garden to Eat Worms	131

Introduction

This little book is dedicated to everyone who has ever tried to write succinctly.

It's not as easy as you might think.

There are a few hardy souls, just like me, dotted around the globe, who have been encouraged, coerced, or blackmailed into writing 100-word stories for Colne Radio's 'Bill's Big Bag of Onions', a show that blends words and music twice weekly for the long-suffering listeners of North-east Essex. What did they ever do to deserve it, one wonders?

To demonstrate how difficult it is to hit that 100-word target precisely, I have made Herculean efforts to keep this…

(Word count: 100)

Love Is a Many Splendored Thing

I fully intended to kick off this personal selection of scribbles with a warm, embracing, romantic gathering of little stories in tribute to 'Love and Marriage'. They are so often gently cuddled together, like peaches and cream, or like milk and honey, or like chalk and cheese.

On second thoughts, perhaps they should be kept quite separate. For 'marriage', see under *'Families – Who'd 'ave 'em'*.

At this juncture, it would be wise for me to point out that any resemblance in these tales to anyone living or dead, is entirely coincidental, especially with regard to those stories that mention wives.

(word count – 100)

Handing Over

I lie here, breathing shallow, eyes closed, no strength to open them.

A hand creeps under the bedcovers and clasps mine with a gentle squeeze. The same hand that once gripped mine as we looked right, looked left, looked right again. The same hand that shook itself from mine to run gleefully into the playground, that I gave away to another man who never loved her as I have done.

And now, that same hand offers a reassuring link to her own children – a touch that passes from generation to generation eternally.

My mother's hand beckons me to rejoin her.

This, like many pieces in this book, is autobiographical. Isn't all writing in some sense? I hope it expresses the love of a father for his daughter and hers for him and reminds us that love is eternal. I could so easily have included it in a section on death. In fact, I was shocked to see how many of my stories revolve around or refer to death in some form. I have deliberately not grouped them all together, but you should spot the theme recurring in many guises. Offers of psychoanalysis or similar professional help welcomed.

Duologue: Part 1: Clocking In

(Female voice)

[SFX: Background bustle of a train station. Men's footsteps approaching.]

"Oh, hello officer… No, I'm fine, I'm waiting for someone… Yes, I know, I've been here nearly an hour. He's late. Perhaps his train was delayed… We met on Tinder, you see. He said we should meet under the clock at Waterloo. Rather old fashioned, I know, but it sounded rather romantic… My name? And number? Oh, for your records. Yes, of course… And this is your card, with your personal phone – in case I need to call you. Thank you."

[SFX: Man's footsteps receding]

Well, he was very dishy. I'll wait another ten minutes then I think someone will be getting a call.

I know - you think I'm cheating already. No, two 100-word stories that are linked together is not really a 200-word story. They can be read and appreciated (I hope) independently. It just so happens that this story and the next work neatly as a pair. So neatly, in fact, that I'm counting them only once towards the 100 stories in this book. Oh, alright, I'm cheating.

Duologue: Part 2: Clocking Out

(Male voice)

[SFX: Background bustle of a busy street. Lady's footsteps approaching.]

"Excuse me, you've just dropped something… That's no problem… The time? Yes, it's nearly 2 o'clock. I should know. I've been here nearly an hour!... Yes, I'm waiting for someone. We met on Tinder. Very modern! We agreed to meet here under the clocktower at King's Cross. It looks like I've been stood up, doesn't it?... Oh, you're waiting too. You're not – no. I see. You were meeting some girlfriends for coffee. *[pause]* I could do with a stiff vanilla latte right now… And you know a place. Of course, you do. Shall we…?"

[SFX: Two sets of footsteps receding. Speech fades out]

"What's your name by the way. I'm…"

SFX means 'sound effects'. It's useful to remember that these stories were written for a listening audience. Try tuning in to Colne Radio on 106.6fm on a Tuesday evening at 8:00pm or Sundays at 10:00pm for the full, audio experience. Also available on a podcast near you.

Grannie Likes to Google

[SFX: mobile phone rings}

"Hello, Grandma."

"David, it's Grandma. I need your advice, darling. You remember Stan – died last year. Well, I've lost Marjory's number. Thought I'd hunt about on Gogglesearch. Anyway, I've found this marvellous app that's specially for old grannies for finding friends – Grindr, I expect you know it, So I've been searching – "

"Grandma, you're not going to find Marjory on Grindr."

"I don't know. I've found your father. Anyway, this very nice young man has been in touch and frankly, David, I don't understand half he's saying to me. So, I want you to interpret. Now then, what's - ?"

[SFX: sound of phone disengaging]

This piece was for a show dedicated to online dating. Now, Grandma isn't looking for love necessarily, but if she's not very careful, she's going to find more of it than she bargained for.

The Train Now Departing

She was beautiful, with her long, blond hair and her captivating smile. I can smell her now. I fell in love on the first day of school. We were 5. I loved her for 10 years, ever hoping that one day we'd be united.

Sixty years later, she was on the platform as I stepped off the train from Colchester.

"Valerie?" I said, "it's you!"

"I have no idea who you are," she said, suspiciously.

"We were at school together."

"I doubt it," she said, stepping onto the train, brushing past, and leaving me with nothing but her lingering aroma.

Special Delivery

It started when she was just 14. Even with her poor mathematical skills, Madelaine computed that this ritual had lasted half her life.

Every year, he brought her a bouquet of red roses and an over-sized, padded card.

She had the door open before the postman's finger touched the bell. Every year, he smiled knowingly, and every year she giggled girlishly as she signed for the packets. He left her with a cheery wave.

Madelaine closed the door, dropped both packages in the bin and resigned herself to waiting another year for her special Valentine delivery from her handsome postman.

The next group of 'love stories' relate the saga of a hapless, lovelorn Valentine, and his pursuit of the unattainable. These were broadcast on or about 14th February each year between 2022 and 2024.

Valentine's Day Card
2022

Valentine cursed his parents most days but never more so than today, 14th February. Determined to avoid the annual ribbing about his name and the jibes at his inability to attract a partner, he decided to spend the day quietly at the British Library.

"Reader's Pass?" asked the pretty, young librarian.

"I don't have one. I just want to spend the one day here."

"OK," she smiled brightly, "I'll issue you with a day card.

There you are. Enjoy your day."

Their fingers touched lightly as she handed over Valentine's day card.

"Thank you." He smiled back. "I'll cherish it."

Tentative Steps

2023

Valentine stood nervously by the steps outside the British Library clutching a single red rose. It was twelve months to the day since their eyes and fingers had met fleetingly across Valentine's one-day library access card.

She was there. She hesitated. Her eyes lit up and she skipped down the steps, a beaming smile on her face, brushed straight past Valentine and fell into the arms of the tall, rugged young man covered in plaster dust standing a few feet away.

Valentine sauntered home alone, wondering if perhaps he'd left it a little too long to pursue his dream girl.

Virginal Valentine's Virtual Vicissitudes

Part 1 - Reflection

2024

As Valentine's Day loomed, virginal Valentine reviewed his recent catalogue of romantic encounters.

It had been an eventful year for him: a birthday peck on the cheek from Daniella in Sales, holding hands with Scarlet from Book Club through the entire screening of Oppenheimer, and what could only be described as a light petting session with Monica at the office Christmas party. But the love of his life, Sonia, the prettiest, most alluring librarian in the British Library, continued to evade him. A dramatic gesture was needed if she were to ever stamp his card. Of course!

♪♪ Moonpig.com ♪♪

Virginal Valentine's Virtual Vicissitudes
Part 2 – Stormy Relationships
2024

A sudden cloudburst forced Valentine into the nearest bus shelter. She was huddled – in tears.

"It's you," he said, "Sonia, from the library."

"Sorry," she stammered, "I see so many faces."

"You're crying"

"I've been stood up. Some idiot sent me a Moonpig Valentine's card at work. Now my boyfriend thinks I'm cheating."

"Oh, sorry." Then, silence, broken only by the clatter of rain and Sonia's tears.

"I'm going to the pub." said Valentine, "Coming?"

"Anywhere dry would be good," she sobbed.

"I'm Valentine."

"How apt! I remember you now."

He took her hand, and they braved the storm together.

Families – Who'd 'ave 'em

I hope this batch doesn't give the impression I'm no lover of family life. Quite the contrary. With six daughters and many grand and great-grandchildren, family life revolves about us in a swirling miasma that obliterates almost every other aspect of life, and yet I love it still.

'Family', of course, is a fluid description. It can mean more than simply blood relations. We live in a world of extended families, broken, distant, lost, and work families, support networks and friends. Whatever description suits you best is exactly what I mean by 'family'. You'll probably recognize your interpretation somewhere here.

(word count – 100)

The Jigsaw Murders

I leaned back in despair and gave up searching for the last straight piece. My wife and her friend were still crouched over the table, focused on the 5,000 piece jigsaw that I'd been given for my birthday.

"Did you read that article about the Jigsaw Murders?" I asked. "The mutilated, dismembered bodies of two women were found scattered over the Scottish Borders. Took them ages to piece them together."

"Why are you telling me this now?" asked my wife, annoyed by the disturbance and revealing the elusive straight piece, clinging resolutely to her left breast.

"Oh, nothing," I mumbled.

This piece could so easily have slotted into a section devoted to murder, death (again) or pastimes, but the inclusion of a family friend, to me, a natural extension to any family, convinces me that this is its proper home.

Grey Tunkle Bill

My Grey Tunkle died today. The day we met was special. I'd never had a Tunkle before. I was eager to know what a grey one was like and excited because I'd been told he belonged to me.

My first impression was a bit of a disappointment. Only his hair was grey and that was just the tufts above his ears. The rest was black or noticeable by its absence. But we soon bonded. He was proud to be my Tunkle, and I was proud to own him.

Goodbye, Grey Tunkle Bill. It was lovely having you all those years.

This is another example of a tale that touches on death. In my defence, this story was written on the day that my Uncle Bill died, which coincided with the day I was diagnosed with Covid and relegated to the guest bedroom with little more than pen and paper, and an infrequent supply of bacon rashers – the only food that could be slid under the firmly bolted door.

Taking the Micky

Micky parked in his usual disabled bay, carefully displayed our long-dead grandfather's blue badge and set off to hunt.

My brother, Micky, the school bully, had grown into a lazy and obnoxious employee, an abusive husband and, thankfully, a mostly absent father.

Currently working as a council parking enforcement officer, he returned at 6:00pm, joyous that he had caught out double his daily quota for the least amount of effort, only to see his battered, and now clamped, Honda Civic being hoisted onto a flatbed. It would cost him £200 or more to get it back.

Oh, how I laughed!

༺༺༺☿༻༻༻

Occasionally, our esteemed producer, Adrian, who is also one of two 'voices' who bring our humble contributions to life on Bill's Big Bag of Onions, *likes to present a themed show. That is, one where the stories, and often the accompanying musical selections, reflect a common theme. Often, we Onionisters are given nothing more than a hint or a word to set us on our way. The theme for which this story was written was schadenfreude.*

The Pies That Came in From the Cold

Gustav the Pie-man turned up his collar against the bitter wind and stared glumly at the grey and formidable Berlin Wall. It had stood for 20 years, solidly and symbolically dividing East from West, brother from sister.

As dusk settled, he carried his display of homemade pretzels back into the shop. Little did the guards know that this signalled that the coast was clear. Seconds later, a silhouette slid silently along an old electricity cable stretched between two buildings either side of the wall and dropped, unhindered, to freedom.

Perhaps, thought Gustav, this one might bring news of his sister.

My thanks to John le Carre, without whom this story could never have been written.

Dessert Island Dicks

The Browns preferred chocolate brownies. The Swiss family, the Robinsons, their Swiss rolls.

It was a feud that had started the day the two families had been shipwrecked on this desert island. Luckily, both men being master bakers and with a year's supply of flour and baking goods washed up with them, they had survived, albeit solely on cake.

But supplies were dwindling fast, and tempers were fraying. It was Victoria Brown who threw the first rock cake.

"I'll get you for that, you little tart!" yelled Robinson.

Now, the two families were facing each other with buns drawn.

"Squirt!"

You will not be surprised to hear that this altercation occurred on a Sundae.

Will This Lunacy Never End?

Michael lost great-grandfathers in the Crimean War.

In 1941, Nazis murdered 30,000 Ukrainian Jews: Michael lost all his remaining family in the Babi Yar Massacre in Kyiv. He was already incarcerated as a prisoner of war then and destined for a similar fate, but he escaped and made his way to England, settling in Colchester after the war and raising a new family.

When Michael died, his family name died with him, but his daughters and grandchildren are proud of their heritage and pray each day for the Ukrainian families trapped in today's bloody turmoil.

Will this lunacy never end?

Sorry, I should have warned you. They're not all light and fluffy.

Let's Twist Again Like We Did Last Christmas

(Christmas 2023)

Where would we be without our Christmas traditions? Auntie Flo's sloe gin, Uncle Albert's home-made egg nog that everyone but Albert surreptitiously pours down the sink. The obligatory family game of Monopoly on a board that had seen better days 20 years ago, that always ends in bitter recriminations and Grandma's cherry brandy induced re-telling of her earliest sexual experience in a seedy hotel on the Old Kent Road.

Well, this year, I'm starting a new tradition. I have secretly replaced the Monopoly board with Twister. That should keep Grandpa awake and will either kill or cure his back problem.

☙❦❧

Christmas is a time for giving, and, if it's in us, for forgiving.

I hope somebody bears that in mind, as the next four mini-sagas home in on that most fundamental aspect of family life – marriage.

Moving Experience

They're right. Moving house is one of the most stressful experiences, second only to losing a loved one, and head and shoulders above divorce. There is so much to remember, so much to do. Solicitors to argue with, estate agents to grit one's teeth over, a million and one organisations to inform, cajole, remind, remind again and finally threaten – to say nothing of the expense. It's a wonder anyone survives it. Looking back, I think I managed it admirably. It's such a pity I forgot to tell the wife.

Ah well, as I say, divorce should be a little easier.

Having experienced all three of these evils multiple times, I am convinced that moving house is by far the worst, although, if I had divorced as many times as I moved (18 so far), it could be a different story. One worthy of selling to the tabloids, methinks.

Does this resonate with you? Isn't it time we did something about it and convinced the great and powerful (solicitors mostly) that the process is much in need of simplification?

How the Other Half Loves

Lord Withers peered over the twin domes of his breakfast eggs and assessed the void between himself and Lady Withers. She poked her egg suspiciously as though it might explode.

What had been his last words to her? "Pass the marmalade, dear," perhaps. It was too long ago to remember.

Satisfied with its veracity, Lady Withers demolished her egg in three deft scoops, quaffed her coffee, rose and left with a haughty, "drawing room if I'm needed".

Withers bent to the task of tackling his eggs, content that at least she was talking to him today.

"Happy Valentine," he mumbled.

Yes, it could have been lumped in with the lovey-dovey ones, but I thought it sat here best.

The Thin End of the Edge Pieces

I'd only done a few edges and was looking forward to some peaceful jigsawing when my wife returned unexpectedly early.

"A jigsaw," she cooed and drew up a chair.

"No," I said.

"What do you mean, no?"

"It's my thing. I prefer to do them on my own."

"Don't be silly," she said, running her fingers through my carefully sorted piles of sky and red bits. "These go here," she said, and seconds later she'd clicked two pieces in place – not even the yellow edge I was working on!

"And that, Your Honour, is where our problems started."

"Divorce granted!"

What is it with me and my obsession with wives and jigsaws? Is there a psychologist in the house?

Sweet Justice

He'd fed me bullshit for most of our married life. I knew it. He knew I knew it and neither of us much cared any more.

His latest 'conference' coincided with his birthday. This year, he's even chosen to spend that day with his beloved secretary than with me. God knows what he sees in her. The only thing they have in common is their peanut allergy.

I've lovingly packed him a small birthday cake. A cake that I'd carefully unwrapped, neatly injected with a hefty dose of peanut oil and painstakingly rewrapped.

Choke on that, the pair of you.

Another themed show; this one titled Revenge Is Sweet. *This time I managed to encompass a number of my favourite topics, love, death and cake. There's a strange lack of jigsaws though. This one was written from the perspective of the woman in the relationship. I expect you spotted that. Perhaps that's why the emphasis is on cake and not jigsaws.*

By the way, grandson 5 (I think they do have names), has a nut allergy. It's not a laughing matter.

A Matter of Life and Death

What is the meaning of life?

I'm of an age when I often ponder the big questions.

Questions like, where are my socks? Why can't I speak to a human being anymore? What is the point of Strictly Come Dancing, and will it never end?

Questions just like these might or might not pop up in the next few pages.

To mitigate the soporific effects of dwelling too long on the meaning of life, the universe and all that stuff, I have interspersed among them one or two ditties on the theme of death. Why are you not surprised?

(word count – 99 – see me)

What Are We Here For?

Aged 10, I stared out of the classroom window musing, "what am I here for?" I should have been out there, playing - kicking a football about.

At 20, office windows beckoned with more carnal dreams, but the sentiment was the same.

Ages 30 to 60 were philosophical: the nature of the universe and our place in it drew me away from the mundane routines of life.

And now? I am in my bedroom, a phone in one hand, a half-drunk cup of tea in the other, and I ask myself, "what did I come in here for?".

Nothing changes.

Look Who It is!

At 18 I was, just once, mistaken for Roger Moore by somebody myopic or confused, or both. Still, it counts.

By 30, my aquiline nose and burgeoning paunch drew comparisons with Ian Botham. Later, a fuller figure, and even fuller beard, saw me referred to more than once as Pavarotti. We'll gloss over that.

Now, clean-shaven and slightly more sylph-like, I am often compared to Peter Sellars. Slightly odd, as he died 40 years ago. Still, I accept it as a compliment.

It's such a shame that I was never famous enough to be recognised for who I actually am.

Who do you think you look like?

Nurture v. Nature

(From the Ridiculous to the Sublime)

I'm pretty sure that I was born upside down; my nose is always running and my feet smell. Also, I was born with a broken arm. My father told me I was hanging on 'til after the wedding.

It's birth traumas like this, and the nine months that go before them, that create the human being that we are destined to become, and all the nurturing, cajoling, privilege, and neglect that we experience thereafter does nothing more than smooth or wrinkle the surface.

How we respond to what happens to us comes from the soul – and that we cannot change.

Hungry for the Sea

This is the tale, the fateful tale,
of Jack Young and his bride.
They chartered a plane for their honeymoon,
but the pilot promptly died.

The plane spun wildly to the sea;
nought left but a broken wing.
To this, Jack Young, his sodden bride
and the poor, dead pilot cling.

For forty days they floated there.
Surely, they could never survive.
But a passing cruise ship picked them up,
and the pair were still alive.

Jack Young would eat no lung.
His wife would eat no spleen.
And so, between them both, you see,
they picked the carcass clean.

It's tough writing stories 100 words long, not 99 or otherwise wrong. Adding rhyme and metre is doubly hard, especially when wanting to write by the yard.

Life

Life has brought me to that age when I stare into the mirror in wonder each morning only to see my grandfather staring back at me, equally perplexed. What happened to the flowing, dark locks and apple cheeks of yesteryear? I wake each day in the fervent hope that pallid has become the new 'in' colour. It never is.

And then I remind myself – each crevice is a cherished memory, and every grey hair was earned on the battlefield of life. Would I swap those memories and experiences for the face and figure of my youth?

Not on your life.

Just Chillin'

I'm sitting here on my favourite bench, in the playing field above my village in North Devon, gazing at the faraway hills and dotted homesteads, and the ribbons of cloud and sea. My cocker spaniel puppy is chasing butterflies and my shih-tzu hovers, never more than 10 feet away, while I dwell on friends lost – by time, by distance, by age, by accident.

The bench is dedicated to another local who also loved this spot, and to his faithful flatcoats. It's inscribed "With best friends there is no such place as faraway".

Excuse me while I chill a little longer.

A poor life this is if, full of care,

We have no time to stand and stare.

from 'Leisure' by W H Davies, 1911

From Little Acorns

He was a mighty oak. Here he'd stood for over 400 years. He'd seen his family felled around him, devoured for houses, furniture, carts, trinket boxes, or simply tossed on fires. The tiny hamlet he'd known as a sapling had grown around him. It's people ageing and dying so quickly it seemed impossible to him that they lived long enough to learn anything. Yet, here he stood, in a town – in the way, a nuisance, an irritant. Forget the hundreds he'd sheltered and fed, the pleasure he'd brought to generations. He was redundant.

He felt the first saw-bite and groaned.

April

I am 16 again and back in the hospital bed where a noxious mixture of illnesses confines me for weeks without end. But today is different. Cajoled by a thoughtful nurse, a visiting ex-patient takes me for a ride in his open-top car "for a spot of fresh air".

Oh joy. Grey from a bleak, debilitating winter, my face is brushed by a gentle, refreshing breeze. The sun tingles my skin, pouring life giving energy back into my broken body. Birds rejoice in the trees, catching the rhythm of the wildflowers dancing in verdant verges.

I shall always love April.

This was from another of those themed shows, this one, not surprisingly, celebrating each month of the year.

It is a true story.

Friendly Fire

Lieutenant Commander Steel cradled his cocoa; small comfort against the bitter sea. It was less than a week into WWII and his sub, the Triton, the Oxley and three others patrolled off Norway. Another sub had surfaced.

"Could be Oxley, but she's out of position. Send a box lamp challenge."

No response – to that or two more challenges.

"Good God!," yelled Oxley's Lieutenant Commander Bowerman, "Now she's sending up flares! Didn't you respond to her signals?!"

"I thought so, sir."

"Well respond now!"

"The equipment's jammed, sir. I can't get…"

Two snake-like, deadly waves sped towards them. Fifty-three lives lost.

And so is this.

It's Not All 9 to 5

This little section explores our lives in work and play.

Whether we earn our crust as barristers, teachers, receptionists or cleaners; whether we work in a shop, a factory or are office-bound, the vagaries of life are destined to track us down.

And when we're not toiling hard at work, the hand of fate will find us just as easily hard at play.

If these tales are anything to go by, my life is full of incidents that make me laugh, because if I didn't, I'd cry.

I laugh in the face of misadventure, pedantry and frustration, Fie on you!

(word count – 100 – better)

Had a Good Day at School, Darling?

We took 150 unruly Colchester schoolchildren to church today, to sing carols. Covid forced us outside, of course, in the rain. The speaker system I took didn't work, no matter how hard I kicked it, so I had to lead the singing from the front – with no music! It was like a really bad, sober karaoke. I even added all the instrumentals.

At the end, I approached the Reverend Wendy with some trepidation. She gripped my sodden hand and smiled sweetly.

"Never mind, dear," she said, "the first Christmas was something of a disaster. Your performance suited the occasion perfectly."

The Archer

They say it takes 10,000 hours to master any skill. Archery is no exception.

Stand square to the boss, feet slightly apart. Secure your arrow in it's nock with the cock facing you. Raise the bow and draw back smoothly – not too far. Kiss the string. Keep still. Is the bow upright? Check your right elbow. Focus on the gold; get that sight exactly right. Breathing – shallow. Relax. Hold for a second or two. Keep still. Release with the right hand. Don't lower the bow too soon, and…

…miss the target completely. Ah well, only another 9,999 hours to go.

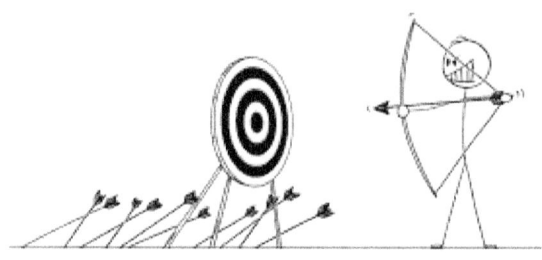

Dress Down Day

I've been taking things too literally just lately – not helpful when you work in Colchester's largest department store.

Last week the Manager said he wanted to see me in Ladies Underwear straight away to explore ideas for a Dress Down Day.

Five minutes later he's drumming his fingers on the tights counter on the third floor while I'm stood in his office on the top floor dressed only in a pair of lacey panties and a bra hastily borrowed from Gladys in White Goods.

Not a good look in an overweight 62-year-old man with knock knees and a pigeon chest.

The Stargazers

Joan and Beryl had been stargazers since junior school. Now, late 40's, married with kids, their passion was still their relentless search for new stars. Every Friday, they met at the local chippy, drove to their favourite, dark, secluded spot and waited.

"Is that -?"

"No."

"Look – there, there!" Joan pointed a greasy finger. "Is that -?"

"Yes," said Beryl, agog, "it's George Clooney."

"Didn't we get him last year?" Joan leafed through her dog-eared exercise book.

"Still, it's better than nothing," said Beryl, popping in another chip as George hopped onto his Vespa and sped away into the night.

A Frosty Receptionist

Molly fished out her gum, clasped it between elegantly manicured thumb and forefinger and accepted line one.

"Branston and Branston, Financial Advisors. How may I help?"

"Is that Branston and Branston, Financial Advisers?" I asked.

"Yes," she said, dropping an octave.

"Good, I'm in a bit of a pickle and – "

Molly had heard this before and was well rehearsed.

"Our advisers are busy," she snapped, cut the call, and returned her gum to its rightful place.

Oh dear, I thought, staring forlornly at the handset. I'll have to look elsewhere for advice about my 100 million euro lottery win.

Give Us a Break

I queued patiently behind several tourists. As they dispersed, I filled the void, but a young couple hurtled in, shouting their demands.

"Were you queuing from the other side?" said the man eventually, feigning innocence. His wife wouldn't even look at me.

"Go ahead," I said magnanimously. "No hurry."

Four hot drinks and four individually cooked chocolate crepes later, I was finally asked for my order.

"One latte, please"

"Oh," he said, laughing, "we should have let you go first."

"It's only been twenty minutes," I said through gritted teeth. Still, she wouldn't look me in the eye.

Bloody grockles.

The Rise and Fall of the Blue Whale

It was Fred's first day at the Natural History Museum. It mattered nothing to him how lowly his position. He was here, at last, free to push his broom from room to room, drinking in its great sweep of history.

And then – disaster. Too intent at marvelling at the exhibition of human evolution, he failed to notice that his broom had snagged one of the stanchions holding up the blue whale skeleton which now dominated Hintze Hall. One sharp tug and 221 bones tumbled noisily to the floor.

For Fred, it was the greatest sweep of history of his life.

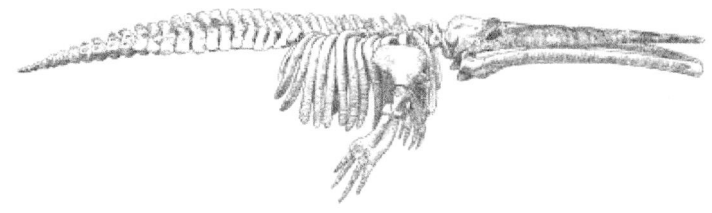

Life's a Beach

...and welcome to Westward Ho! beach's annual 'Who Can Squeeze the Biggest Bottom into the Smallest Bikini' competition, with more entrants than ever, gathering in their hundreds from all over the world.

The competition was wide open this year but there wasn't a Brazilian in sight. The bronze medallion went to Ali from Algeria in her tan coloured, tassled, two-piece, just losing out to Mona from Monaco who snatched silver in her sexy, semi-sheer sequined set. Stewards are still arguing over the unexpected gold awarded to Bill from Billericay in the first ever entry in a loose-fitting, gold lamé mankini.

Please supply your own picture.

Morning Gloria

Meanwhile, in carriage 3, seat 12 (his favourite), Jerry sat pondering his daily morning routine. Rise at 6:27, the optimum time to gain sufficient sleep and breakfast, shave, shower and dress in time for the 7:19, 27a bus to the station. Then, allowing 5 minutes for unforeseen delays, hopping onto the 7:44 from Colchester to Liverpool Street, arriving at 8:49 (but invariably 8:52) leaving precisely 8 minutes for a brisk walk to the office and, time permitting, 10 seconds to look in on Gloria for a breezy "Good morning" before settling at his desk – at Transport for London's Timetabling Department.

Near and Far

It is reliably reported that most accidents happen in your home and that most road traffic collisions occur within a mile of your house. Consequently, I am moving in with my Auntie Muriel, who lives over three miles away. I will be much safer there.

The following foreshortened fables compare and contrast the charisma of Colchester with a tantalising taste for travel.

It seems to me that either choice is fraught with hurdles if the experiences recounted here are anything to go by.

I hate to give away showbiz secrets, but very few of us 'Onionistas' actually live in Colchester!

(word count – 100 – doing very well)

Holiday Romances, Essex Style

Lucinda married Wayne and promptly produced Percival and Waynetta. Tracy married Jeremy and promptly produced Darren and Fiona. Both marriages made in haste rather than heaven, it seems.

Divine intervention came with the double booking of a Spanish villa. By day two, Lucinda and Jeremy were off exploring relics while Wayne and Tracy lazed, poolside, keeping half an eye between them on the kids.

Some minor luggage juggling found Lucinda, Jeremy, Percival and Fiona returning to a chocolate-box cottage in Halstead, while Tracy, Wayne, Waynetta and Darren headed for Tilbury, both sets eagerly awaiting their first annual reunion in Spain.

Brief Encounters

I briefly commuted daily into London, sometimes rubbing shoulders with minor celebrities, like David Soul, the taller half of Starsky and Hutch. We were trapped, sardine-like, rubbing shoulder to elbow. We didn't talk.

I sat opposite Paul Ross, brother of the more famous Jonathon, his ear to a phone, my nose in a book. We didn't talk either.

There was a buffet-car rendezvous with actor, Michael Robbins, slurping lager, studying a script while I concentrated on my crossword. We didn't talk.

So many brief encounters, but did we speak? No, we didn't. I sometimes wish I wasn't quite so British.

Mildred

Mildred Micklewhite wasn't born to be a Mildred; she'd had Mildredness thrust upon her. She blamed her mother entirely. The fact there'd been Mildreds in her mother's line for 16 generations was neither relevant nor verifiable.

It was November in her 45th year before she resolved the problem. She'd make herself inescapably famous.

She mustered everything she needed: a sharp knife, cheese wire, gloves, a woolly scarf in case it got chilly, and a small pot of that stuff they use on rats.

Waiting for the 104 bus into Colchester, she fondly pictured tomorrow's headline: Mildred Micklewhite – Manningtree's Mundane Murderer!

The Godfather of all Journeys

Italian trains are confusing.

Our journey entailed a change at Naples. When Vesuvius passed us on the wrong side, we knew we'd caught the wrong train, but that was after we'd thrown a dapper young man out of 'our' reserved seats. I also deduced the bulge under his jacket was not a hernia, and his two bulging 'friends' were probably not just mates.

In faltering Englitalian, we apologised profusely. He made a call. The train stopped especially for us at the next station and his henchmen helped us off with our luggage.

With broad smiles they carried on to Sicily.

Talking Types Let Us Down Again

So, how unhappy must you be to want to move to Colchester? We surveyed 100 people who have moved here in the past year.

Bob from Greenstead said, "I'd just been through a divorce, then my Mum died, and I was made redundant. I was pretty damn low, but then I won a competition in a newspaper for a brand-new house. I moved in three months ago and, quite frankly, I wish I'd never bought that bloody paper."

And Doris, in Wivenhoe, said, "I've never been happier, but then, I've always been a grumpy old sod."

There you have it.

In December 2022, it was announced by the Office for National Statistics that Colchester was officially the unhappiest place in Britain with an average happiness score of 6.8 out of 10.

Colchester is the home of Colne Radio and its flagship programme, Bill's Big Bag of Onions.

I leave you to draw your own conclusions.

Dangerous Cornering by J B Priestlike

Maud was my sat-nav buddy for years, guiding me through country lanes and urban mazes with her calm, slightly alluring voice. Today, she was advising me to "turn left at the next junct –" when some brash, young, Australian guy burst in.

"No mate, go right, it's quicker."

"Turn left at the next junction," repeated Maud, unperturbed.

"Right! Ignore her - go right."

I turned right.

Maud has gone and I'm now in the hands of this strange, insistent Aussie. I have no idea where I am, how I'll get home or if Maud will ever come back to me.

This story was prompted by a lengthy session of listening to the entire works of J B Priestley in an effort to a) keep up with student studying one of his plays and b) learn from a master playwright. Judging by this story, it was rather a waste of time.

Downstage With Feeling

Remember your lines, speak clearly, and don't fall over the furniture. Simples!

Cast as the comedy vicar in Ayckbourn's Gosforth's Fete in a semi-professional production for Colchester's Arts Festival, I hid my poor grasp of the script behind a Nimmo-like, stuttering delivery.

When I stubbed a toe on a trestle table and hurtled downstage at enormous speed clutching a steaming mug of coffee in each hand it brought howls of laughter from most of the audience and of anguish from two old ladies in the front row.

Quite the funniest thing I've seen at the Mercury said one local journalist.

Another theatre-based story quite so soon?! That wasn't very good planning.

Sláinte – Good Health!

A little advice, as if it's needed; when wooing the beauty destined to be your next wife, it's prudent not to tell her, after your first date, that you cannot meet next weekend as you're flying to Dublin to see your ex-wife, no matter how justifiable the reason.

Never fear, the Gods wreaked their gastronomic vengeance.

Just landed, we stopped at the first proper Irish pub for my first proper Irish Guinness. I spent the next two days in such agony I was convinced I'd drunk straight from the Liffey.

I still love Guinness though – and the beautiful new wife.

Please make a note of this page number, just in case my wife rings.

Never Work with Children and Animals

This is sound advice if you're a TV presenter, rock god or A-listed film star. For the rest of us, and, forgive me for assuming, but I guess that includes you, working with children and animals is as unavoidable as endless adverts on ITVX – only possible if you pay.

For 'work' read 'live'.

They smell awful, leave messes, won't come when they're called, and are constantly hungry yet never eat what you give them.

Animals are no better.

This collection celebrates the wonderful worlds of children and animals. You can skip it if you think it might be too painful.

(word count – 100 – you're just showing off now)

Angling for Success

"Martin, stop!"

Martin's elbow froze. A wisp of smoke hovered between them.

"You're not good at this, are you?"

"It wasn't my choice, Miss."

"It was. Last term I said you could do carpentry or metal-working this year. You chose carpentry."

"I thought it were something to do with fishing, Miss." Martin's elbow disappeared in another blur.

"Stop - there'll be nothing left! Show me what you've done."

The carbonised remains of Martin's sandpaper drifted listlessly to the floor.

"Well, that's — lovely, Martin. It's — very… It looks a bit - fishlike, Martin. What would you call it?"

"A carp, Miss."

Pronoun'cing Their Names

Within minutes of the twins being born she said, "we must call them Lesley and Pat".

"Which is which?" I asked. "We have a boy and a girl."

"You can't say that!" she screeched. "You can't force genders on them.

"But one of them's got a – "

"Stop!"

"And the other one's got – "

"It doesn't work like that anymore. They are 'theys' – genderless. It doesn't matter who is Lesley or Pat. When they grow up, they can choose which gender they want to be, or not."

So that is how we settled on their names – Toby and not Toby.

Chiumbo's First Christmas, 1899

(phonetically Chee-oom-bo)

Chiumbo, the goat-watcher, squatted on the ridge above the Enkara Nyrobi swampland watching them building the strange metal road to world's end. Labourers – sweat glistening on their ebony backs. White men – joking about as usual.

A shape moved slowly towards Chiumbo – three men on camels, one dressed in red, his sun-bleached face masked by a bushy, white beard. A soldier?

Chiumbo rose, gripping his spear. If they wanted goats, he'd die first. He was a man now – 12.

They stopped. Chiumbo raised his spear. They laughed, dropped a package at Chiumbo's feet, and moved on, chanting, "Happy Christmas, little one".

Chiumbo means 'little' in the Bantu language and is found as a boy's name among the Mwera people. This tale was written for a Christmas edition of Bill's Big Bag of Onions that gathered Christmas stories from around the world.

Alice's Lost Adventure

Quite frankly, Alice was bored. She had tried following her sister's finger as it meandered line by line through her uninspiring book, but it had not improved the story. Why grown-ups insisted on reading books without pictures quite befuddled her.

Alice closed her eyes and listened instead to the gentle breeze stirring the long grass and the incessant chatter of insects and distant birdsong.

Seconds later, she was being shaken by the shoulder and admonished roundly for being so rude as to fall asleep.

What a shame, thought Alice, I'm sure I was on the brink of a wonderful dream.

Written with much affection for the esteemed Rev. Charles Lutwidge Dodgson, otherwise known as Lewis Carroll.

Oh, my ears and whiskers!

Animal Instincts

I hare about, beavering away, buzzing from one thing to another, my butterfly mind unable to settle. I have the concentration of a goldfish. I'm too dogmatic, and a catastrophe in a crisis - like a bull in a china shop.

"Stop horsing around!" my wife says, but I'm a rabbit caught in headlights.

I'm a bear with a sore head when I'm hungry, until I wolf down a big meal and feel as fat as a pig.

I suppose I'll be like it 'til the day I croak. A leopard can't change his spots.

Ah well, I'm only human.

Dear Santa

"Why are you putting my letter up there?" asked Jimmy.

"When Santa comes down, he'll find it." said Daddy. "He'll reach inside his magic sack and pull out your present."

"We saw the man in the red suit yesterday and I said I want a fire engine."

"But he can't remember everything, so we put a letter up the chimney on Christmas Eve to remind him."

That night, as Jimmy slept, they lit a fire. The letter, now aflame, caught the chimney alight. Jimmy couldn't believe his luck. He got his fire engine, and eight red suited Santas delivered it.

Hoomins is Weird

Hoomins is weird. They make weird squeaky noises wot makes no sense and don't care if attackers come to our camp, then when I tell them attackers come, they shout and hide me in a cage!

Yesterday, they bringed me two new fluffy toys that is for playing rat killing and 'stick your nose in' and sleeping on and we had good game called 'him trying to get them and me not letting him', 'til he made big growly noise.

Today, he's hidden them on the end of his legs as if I can't sniff them out.

Hoomins is weird.

The Pragmatist's Fairy Tales
by the Grim Buggers

Once upon a time there were three Billy Goats Gruff. They went trip-trap, trip-trap over the rickety, rackety bridge. It was the troll's day off.

Once upon another day there were three little pigs. One built his house of straw, one of sticks and one of bricks. They lived happily ever after because the local wolf was Jewish.

Once upon the very next day there were three bears: big, old Daddy Bear, medium-sized Mummy Bear and teeny-weeny Baby Bear. They lived in a cave and Goldilocks had too much damn sense to go poking around in bears' caves.

THE END

What Goes Up Must Come Down

The Kenyan sun rose gently, banishing the cool of night and bathing all it touched with a warm, golden glow.

Our balloon inflated quickly as its burners exploded into life and soon we were floating high above the Masai Mara, as breathless as the wind that bore us.

Wildebeest scattered aimlessly, oblivious to the lions lazing among the jacarandas. Queues of elephants plodded towards morning waterholes. Gazelle and hyenas mingled harmoniously, every beast at peace with itself and each other.

Sadly, hundreds died later that day, when a city of termite mounds saved us from an unplanned visit to Tanzania.

Ineptitude and Politics

So many of my short stories revolve around ineptitude, incompetence and misadventure that I thought the subject deserved a section to itself.

Did I say earlier that much of my writing is autobiographical? Well, that doesn't apply to this section, of course. (Although, to be perfectly fair, I could quite legitimately have entitled this volume 'Tales of Ineptitude, Incompetence and Misadventure' and saved myself a lot of work trying to sift them into categories.)

I also had a handful of stories with a political bias and decided that this group of stories was undoubtedly their natural home. I say no more.

(word count – 101 – that was deliberate, wasn't it!)

Humboldt

Humboldt was fed up with being bullied. If it wasn't his name, it was his glasses, horn-rimmed and patched together with a faded, pink plaster. Then it was his braces. Later still, his admittedly unprepossessing face.

By age 17, friendless, partnerless, and with no great ambition to press himself forward either socially or professionally, his mother decided that joining a karate club would be the ideal solution for him. It would toughen him up, widen his social circle and, with any luck, improve his confidence.

May God rest his soul.

Well, that wasn't much of a eulogy thought his mother.

☙☙☙♉☙☙☙

Cabinet Reshuffle

Boris closed the door on another difficult week. The Indian variant had threatened to scupper his roadmap to New Normal. Israel and Palestine had swapped bricks for mortars in a parody of daily life in the Commons. Rounding it off, there was more mud-slinging about sleaze and corruption to dodge. This demanded a cabinet reshuffle. It wouldn't solve anything, but he'd feel better.

By midnight the task was done. Tomorrow, he would wake refreshed and eager to start again. He'd just have to remember that now his socks would be in the bottom drawer, and his underwear in the top.

This one was clearly written at a time when Boris was our illustrious Prime Minister but, as we know, history has a habit of repeating itself, and will be true for any name you wish to replace it with.

A Position of Trust

Trusted consultants like myself, when working for the Metropolitan Police, are issued security tags to avoid being escorted to their desks by burly policemen. After two weeks, I was summonsed to Scotland Yard, interrogated, photographed and dismissed with a shiny new card pinned to my chest and strict instructions to guard it.

200 yards later, tube doors closing behind me, I glanced down to admire the void where my proud acquisition should be.

Aaaaargh!

Twenty frantic minutes later, I was back at Scotland Yard sheepishly explaining my ineptitude.

Unsurprisingly, it was another six weeks before I was granted a replacement.

Order! Order!

It had been one of the longest parish council meetings on record. Harsh words had been exchanged. Blame and denial battled for supremacy. Occasional meek calls for calm and tolerance from the Chair were lost in the maelstrom of the bitter argument.

Perpetually red-faced Councillor Winfred Digby-Jones resigned in disgust – twice. The Vice-Chair and the Clerk even challenged each other to pistols at dawn.

Finally, some order was restored. It had been a hard-fought battle, but democracy had found a way. Agreement was reached; the motion finally passed. For future meetings, the refreshments would include both bourbons AND custard creams.

Having spent 13 years as a Parish Clerk to three different parishes, I can assure you that there is more than a hint of realism to this ditty.

The Green Room at the BBC

All that for 3 minutes on a BBC TV documentary!

There's Ernie and Jasmine, Double Trouble, matching jackets. If they're pretending they're identical twins, one shouldn't be female!

Lance, starched GI uniform, doing Wooden Heart again - matches his acting.

Tom's gone Blue Hawaii – tope shirt – tope!? And that lei's wilting.

Adrian - super King Creole leather jacket, but the hair! There'll be no boot black left in his house.

Dennis aimed for Jailhouse Rock but missed. More like Dennis the Menace.

They're calling. Got everything? White jump suit, gold cape – check. Medallions – check. Blast! Forgot my blue suede shoes!

This episode of Bill's Big Bag of Onions followed the exploits of an Elvis impersonator with a series of linked stories and suitable linking Elvis tracks. Well worth a listen if you can catch it on a podcast of your choice.

Boris in Blunderland

(with affectionate regard to the Reverend Charles Lutwidge Dodgson)

"The time has come," the Boris said,
"to talk of many things;
Of Cummings' trips and gravlax,
of partying and flings."

"But wait a bit", the voters cried,
"before we have our chat,
Most of us are quite fed up,
and everyone hates that."

"I weep for you," the Boris said,
"I deeply sympathise."
With crocodile tears he organised
those for the largest prize,
Holding his pocket-handkerchief
before his lying eyes.

"Voters," said the Cabinet,
"we've had a pleasant run.
Shall we rely on you again?"
But answer came there none.
And this was scarcely odd because
they'd cheated every-one.

One to Bind Them All (New Year 2023)

This year, I shall not be making a raft of resolutions to flounder in the unrelenting sea of life. No, this year there will be but one resolution – one to bind them all. Making one resolution that I can keep forever will boost my confidence and self-esteem. I shall sleep with an untroubled mind, be more energised, more able to exercise and shed a few pounds. I shall be happier in myself and, therefore, with others. Yes, one, achievable resolution is the way forward.

I resolve never to make any New Year's resolutions ever again.

There, I feel better already.

ooOoo

Stealing Resolve (New Year 2024)

My track record on New Years' resolutions leaves much to be desired. My history is littered with broken promises, unused gym memberships, unopened slimming magazines and unending lists of uncontacted friends and family.

But this year, I can celebrate. Last year's resolution has been fulfilled and I feel so much better for it. On 1st January last, I resolved not to make any New Year resolutions ever again and – so far so good.

Only one day to go and I will have kept my resolve for one whole year. I shall make the same resolution for next year – oh, bugger!

To Speak or Not to Speak, That is the Question

It is my habit when alone in the car to recite some poetry or Shakespeare pieces that I've committed to memory simply for my own enjoyment. Usually, I muse on these silently as I navigate our country lanes. Sometimes, when the muse takes me, I recite them out loud. Occasionally, when feeling exuberant, I give them full voice, with every inflection perfected.

I was nearing the end of 'To Be or Not To Be' yesterday when my bluetoothed phone told me I had "15 seconds recording time left".

I wonder which friend is wondering who left such a strange message.

An Inspector Falls by J B Priestlike

SCENE: *the drawing room of an Edwardian household. Father leans nonchalantly, one elbow resting on an Adam fireplace. In his hand is a glass of champagne. His wife, son and daughter are seated on separate armchairs, each also holding champagne glasses.*

FATHER: "To our success!"

A knock at the door. They wait patiently. A few moments later a maid enters up right, curtseying.

MAID: "It's a police inspector, Sir."

FATHER: "Show him in –"

The inspector enters, trips over the maid's foot, his hat flying in one direction while he sprawls wildly in the other.

The audience hoots with laughter.

Science or Fiction?

I sometimes think my poor grasp of scientific fact and my sketchy encounters with science fiction merge to create a noodle soup-like belief in what could be termed 'science faction'.

You'll see what I mean as you wade your way through this ramen concoction that lies some way west of 2001: A Space Odyssey and equally east of $E = MC^2$.

You'll find among this heady broth a few Covid inspired anecdotes. To me, that is a period of our lives that now seems but a dim and distant past. I'm sorry if any of these stories recapture unwanted memories.

(word count – 100)

A Hole in One's Theory

Dear Diary. Today, I invented a time machine.

It was easier than I expected, just a couple of batteries, Dad's old pocket watch and a few odd bits from the shed. Anybody could do it. Physics though, eh? What a taskmaster! I mean, I know there has to be laws but, surely, there should be some room for experimentation, some leniency for the odd little mistake. Nobody uses black holes anyway, do they? Who's going to miss one tiny, little one.

Not sure what I'm going to do about tomorrow, though, as it appears there isn't going to be one.

Infinity

A moment of your time. Infinity, let's agree, has no end or beginning. The universe, we agree, is infinite. So, is there more than one universe? Two, for example. If both are infinite, they occupy the same space and time, which our, admittedly basic, grasp of physics states is impossible. The same applies for any number greater than two, including, we conclude, an infinite number of universes.

Ergo, there must be only one. But one is a finite number and infinity insists on no finite numbers. Ergo, (there's that word again) the universe does not exist.

Are you still there?

Flapdoodle

Today's word is FLAPDOODLE.

You are hereby instructed, by order of Her Majesty's Ministry of Interactive Communication, to use the word FLAPDOODLE at least once in every conversation for the next 24-hour period. Failure to employ the word FLAPDOODLE may result in a fine of £100 and serial miscommunicators may be subject to imprisonment not exceeding 30 days.

Remember – today's word is FLAPDOODLE.

(This communication has been vetted and approved by COVID, the Central Office for Vocabularial Improvement and Declension. Any errors in grammar or syntax should be reported to your local COVID office without delay.)

Do not forget – FLAPDOODLE!

Plumbing the Depths

Had a new shower installed last Thursday. Surprised to discover that it's also a portal to another dimension. I only found out when a rather handsome young man stepped out of it asking to use my loo. A severe shortage of plumbers in the fourth dimension apparently.

I wouldn't mind, but it's happened four times this week. Now I'm scared to use it in case he pops up when I'm busy washing my bits.

This quantum mechanics business is all well and good, but I do wish these young students would get their priorities right. Plumbing matters too, you know.

Archie Mead's Principle

Archie Meads thought of himself as an original thinker. It was his wont, daily, to settle into his favourite armchair to ruminate on mankind's problems.

Today, his attention was drawn to his digestive as he carefully dipped it in his steaming tea. See how the liquid is drawn upwards until a critical point is reach... Damn, half a biscuit floated dismally and all too briefly, then tipped and disappeared beneath the surface as gracefully and irretrievably as the Titanic.

"Eureka!," thought Archie, surely every make of biscuit could be identified by its buoyancy.

I bet nobody's thought of that before.

The Little Prick

"You're not going to stick that in me, are you?" she asked in genuine concern. She was young, but surely not that naïve. I smiled reassuringly. Our eyes locked in mutual understanding, and I knew I'd won her over.

Her slender fingers slid aside the flimsy fabric of her dress, exposing her virginal, white skin. She closed her eyes in eager anticipation.

"All done."

"What?" she said, "I didn't even know you'd started."

"Sit and rest for 15 minutes, then you can go home. See you in 12 weeks."

"Not if I can help it," she mumbled. "You little prick."

Here We Go Again

The sun rose, as it had for 5 billion years, fuelling the Earth, cleansing, rebuilding. It had taken only 100 years to smother and repair the carnage of the humans.

The pod touched down, scorching the earth. The crew had known only life on their space station, learning earth's history, the dates of its wars, the names of its dictators and despots, its industries, inventions, and weapons. No-one had yet experienced fresh air or birdsong or felt the warm sun on their face.

The pod doors opened. The Admiral tapped my shoulder. "Take care, the earth is an evil place".

Microcosmic Musings

It's a well-known (possibly fake) fact that, if the empty space between and within our atoms were removed, the entire human race would fit into a space the size of a sugar cube. So, to an electron, is the distance to the next nearest atom like that from Earth to Alpha Centauri? Is our universe simply a microcosm of something much more vast? A God perhaps – or a dog? Who knows? And are there billions of super universes existing in their own concept of time and space, and are they just the microcosmic elements to something even greater – ad infinitum?

The Dawn of a New Age

What a momentous day! The dawning of a new age – 29th March 2021. Let us give thanks by marking this day each year with joyous celebration, dancing in the streets, song and laughter on our lips. We can meet friends for coffee and socially distanced elbow bumps. We can enjoy the great outdoors with members of our family (who will have aged dramatically since last we met). Run up the flags! Let there be praise to whomever God rocks your boat.

But not just yet, eh? I'm pulling the covers over my head. Let's enjoy the peace a little longer.

Dear Self

Dear Self, I write me in the knowledge that this finds you in better spirits than it leaves me.

Our obsession with binary particles has, or should I say 'will', result in absolute disaster. The discovery that all events occur concurrently and our unceasing efforts to harness that knowledge has/will lead not simply to what you currently describe as time travel (a gross misnomer, I add) but also to an understanding of our ultimate destiny. It's not great. We're better off in sublime ignorance.

Desist all research forthwith and concentrate your energies on wine, women and song.

Yours eternally, You.

This rather confusing note was part of a show dedicated to 'advice to my younger self'.

It's Only Natural

Neil languished in his favourite chair, the sickly, sweet smell of his smoke of choice lingering like an old friend who'd outstayed his welcome.

"I'm pondering," he said, "the strange charm of the quark".

"What's a quark" I asked, "apart from the sound a posh duck makes?"

"They are the most fundamental constituents of everything," said Neil, "and yet we cannot see them, hear them, touch them or taste them – rather like tiny Gods that bind us and everything that exists together in oneness."

This was written for a special edition of Bill's Big Bag of Onions that featured the music of Neil Finn of Crowded House fame.

Time and Time Again

It was 31st December at the Reform Club. Messrs Wells and Doyle were locked in convivial mental combat with Monsieur Verne.

"Zere is no zientific evidence for travel s'rough time," said Jules. "Vereas, physics says zat man vill travel to ze moon."

A waiter bringing cognacs tripped, dropped his tray, and released a most ungentlemanly expletive.

"Au contraire," said Wells, contrarily. "I resolve to provide scientific proof within one year."

It was 31st December. Wells, Doyle and Verne exchanged opinions again.

"Ah, cognacs," said Wells. "In precisely 5 seconds, our waiter will trip, drop his tray and…"

(*SFX: CRASH OF FALLING TRAY AND A THUMP*)

"Bugger!"

"Mon Dieu!"

The Mystical and the Magical

I have always been lured by the mystery of magic and the magical pull of mysticism, as this section will attest.

Unlike almost every magician you see Tik-Tokking, Instagramming and Faceaching these days, I do not hold with the giving away of age-old secrets. Nor do I hold with deception and chicanery. It's a dilemma and its horns are pricking me.

You will not find any secret codes among these jottings to reveal any of life's hidden meanings. Nor do I passionately proclaim belief in the afterlife, ghosts, ESP or any religion. I just find the whole thing vaguely interesting.

(word count – 100)

A Magic Cure?

And here we have a plain and simple box. As you can see - completely empty. I spin it – solid - one way in, and I assure you, one way out. I need the assistance of one person from the audience. You sir – yes, you in the blue suit and the cheesy grin. Thank you. And your name is? Paul. Excellent, something short and snappy for the headstone. Now then, just step in here, please. That's it, mind your head. We mustn't damage the equipment, must we? (muffled) And now, I say the magic words...

Bugger, just remembered I'm claustrophobic.

I went to the doctor the other day. I said, "sometimes, I feel like a wigwam, and sometimes I feel like a marquee." He said, "You're too tense".

(T. Cooper – every day of his life)

Unwanted Visitors

I hear the shuffle of feet on the porch, muffled, ethereal voices, the rattle of chains and the ominous click of the lock. The door swings open, slowly creaking on its ancient hinges.

I shrink further into the shadows as stagnant air swirls a million particles of dust through the strip of light that glares across the room. I flinch as it almost touches me.

"You're not seeing it at its best, but this old place will be ideal for a young couple like yourselves."

"It's very cold," says the young woman, shivering in the sunlight.

They all say that.

Lady Felicity Small

It is with joy and anticipation that I announce the passing of Lady Felicity Small, the noted clairvoyant. Her catchphrase 'Small by name, Medium by nature' will invigorate budding spiritualists for many years to come.

Despite blossoming into a double-XL in latter years, Lady Small remained a staunch medium throughout her life, remembered chiefly for channelling the music of Brahms and Liszt, those deeply moving conversations with Napoleon and, of course, her numerous sightings of Elvis Presley.

A séance will be held in Colchester's Charter Hall on Sunday next when it is hoped that Lady Small will be ectoplasmically present.

BILL: Lady Small eagerly awaits the arrival of her husband, Sir Hugo Small, KCB and Bart, her son Timothy 'Tiny Tim' Small and their 12 toy poodles.

This programme was a series of obituaries. Each one was followed by a tailpiece read by the programme's regular presenter, Bill Lawrence – who puts the Bill in Bill's Big Bag of Onions.

It's All Done With Smoke and Mirrors

Another tricky problem for the Lone Ranger and Tonto. How to capture a dozen bank robbers with the posse hours behind them.

"Tonto, stay this end of this narrow canyon and signal when the gang's inside."

"Yes, Kemosabe."

The Lone Ranger galloped to the other end and waited until he saw Tonto's smoke signal. One kick from Silver was all it took. A landslide filled the canyon's narrow exit. He signalled back to Tonto using his shaving mirror and, between them, kept the robbers trapped until help arrived.

"Well," said the Sheriff, "looks like you've performed your magic yet again."

"Hi Yo, Silver, Away!"

Seven

HIM: "Seven has always been a mystical number. God created the heaven and the earth in six days and on the seventh he rested. Some call this the Sabbath Day."

HER: "Others call it B&Q day, or IKEA day."

HIM: "Islam believes in seven levels of heaven and seventh heaven is the ultimate desire for the afterlife, attained only by the most pious."

HER: "In 1965 I came seventh in the sack race, out of eight. I counted that as a win."

HIM: "So don't let anyone tell you that seven is not mystically significant."

HER: "Last night I had a seven-course meal. It was heavenly.

Crime and Punishment

Goodness, that sounds almost good enough to be the title of a book.

When you set out to write the occasional 100-word story, you do not plan to write to a pattern, or to a limited number of themes. You write either whatever pops into your head, (for some of us that can be a dangerous pastime) or you write to order. When Adrian says he wants to do a show about trees, you write a story about a tree. It's only later that you realise that your story about a tree is actually a story about death.

Another pre-occupation that seems to emerge as an underlying theme of mine is crime. I suppose, like most of us today, I am bombarded through television, film and books by the wages of sin, by stories of crime and criminals, police procedurals and 'fly on the wall' documentaries about life's seedy underbelly.

Almost every play and book that I have written features a crime of some sort, from theft, through assault and rape to the wholesale massacre of most of the characters.

It would be a crime not to include a few examples in this collection.

(word count – 194 – absolutely criminal)

Fall from Grace

Pathologist, Grace Johnson, poked at the gaping, splintered wound on the back of the girl's head. She had been struck with force by something sharp. Or perhaps she had struck something during her fateful journey between the top of the multi-storey and the concrete path where now she sprawled untidily.

Looking up, Grace spotted the perfect candidate directly overhead, a protruding brick. That will do. Thank you rain for removing any corroborating evidence. And you'll never tell, will you, Jenny? And you'll never cross me again.

"Any thoughts?" asked Inspector Robins.

"Oh, suicide I think you'll find, Inspector. Definitely suicide."

Sins of the Father

Reverend Barber stared disconsolately at a flickering, blank screen. He had determined that this week's sermon would encompass the seven deadly sins. Where to start? His bulging, 42" elasticated trousers relegated gluttony to a walk-on part and the brand new Ford S-Max glinting on the driveway dared him to talk at any length about greed. Lust? Ah, there he was on firmer ground. Maud would never talk. Hmm – on reflection. Pride? Envy? Wrath? Well, who has never blown up over some small trifle?

"Oh, I can't be bothered," he thought, and settled back on the sofa for his afternoon nap.

The Best Laid Schemes

Lenny looked at Sid. Sid looked at Ernie. Ernie looked at Jack. They nodded. The plan was a good one. They'd been through it a dozen times. Jack and Ernie on lookout back and front, ready to create a diversion if needed. Sid would jemmy the lock on the skylight and help Lenny to haul himself out when the job was done. Lenny would be in and out with the goods in seconds.

"Come on kids, teas on the table!" Lenny's Mum's teas were famous. They shot down the stairs. The lollies in the freezer would still be there tomorrow.

Look out for Lenny, Sid, Ernie and Jack. They grow up, and they walk among us.

This Little Piggy

This little piggy went to market. He's no ordinary shopper, he's the resource finder. He'll find anything you need for your next job.

This little piggy stayed home. The thinker; quiet but important, nonetheless. Need a new idea, or your next job planned? He's your man.

This little piggy had roast beef. The strong one; you want him by your side when the going gets tough.

This little piggy had none. Wiry, fast; in and out with the goods in no time.

And this little piggy went wee, wee, wee - the bleedin' grass. We shot him. Anyone for sausages?

༄༄༄༄༄༄༄༄

This is my favourite 'boiling' of an onion. What you've been reading are raw onions, which is enough to bring a tear to anyone's eye. But Adrian, our multi-talented producer, voice-artist, musicologist, and chief onion boiler, takes those raw onions and boils them for presentation over the air. This one can be found on episode 631 of Bill's Big Bag of Onions from August 2022, which features only onions by me, and has been repeated a couple of times on later, compilation shows.

Do try to find it. It's a treat for the ears.

The Gumshoe

I thought it'd be a piece of cake. All I had to do was finger the bad apple and I'd bring home the bacon. I'm a smart cookie but for a couch potato like me it was a hard nut to crack. I interrogated the big cheese, the chef; thought he was the cream of the crop, but he was nobody's cup of tea. We got on like chalk and cheese. A case that should have been my bread and butter quickly went pear-shaped. I was in a pickle.

In a nutshell, as a gumshoe, I don't cut the mustard.

All that food and no cake?!

Inviting Displeasure

I billed it on the Dark Web as the greatest convocation of pranksters, scammers and con-artists the world would ever see. For just £50.00, a secret conference, attracting the best snake-oil merchants, would offer something new for everyone – a sure opportunity to learn, first-hand, the latest scams.

The day dawned. Tickets had sold like hot cakes. They poured into the O2 from every corner of the globe, yes, even from the darkest bowels of Colchester. But the arena was just an empty shell. Just 20,000 tricksters, milling about, confused, deflated, and wondering if they'd ever get their fifty quid back.

Wouldn't it be great if this really happened?

Claude the Burglar

They called him The Cat, The Night Prowler, The Shadow. There was no drainpipe he could not shin up, no obstacle he could not outwit, no lock he could not pick, no safe he could not crack.

The grand hotels and fine houses of Europe were his playground for 30 years and he grew rich on their pickings.

Claude retired to a quiet corner of Northeast Essex to indulge his lifelong passion for all things feline where he opened a rescue centre for cats. Three months later, he died from sepsis and multiple organ failure induced by cat scratch fever.

Puffed Out

(The Perfect Crime)

"There is no such thing as the perfect crime, Watson."

"I beg to differ, Holmes. I believe I have already perpetrated it."

"Poppycock!" said Holmes dismissively, carefully restoking his pipe. "Every action, criminal or not, leaves its mark. For example, I deduce that you breakfasted on bacon and eggs. I detected an aroma of bacon fat when you entered this morning and that tell-tale yellow stain above your vest pocket was absent when you departed last evening."

"Right again, Holmes!"

Holmes lit a splinter from the fire and sucked smugly on his Meerschaum, drawing the cyanide directly into his lungs.

Why Conan Doyle didn't ask me in first place I'll never know. All this nonsense about falling down a waterfall. It was obvious the fellow would climb out again. I could have killed the irritating little know-all at the stroke of a pen.

Knuckles Malone

Act natural, that's what me old man always said.

Liverpool Street, then the tube. Meet the other boys outside Bank Station. Should have time for a lager top and a pasty at The Westminster – just like old times.

Bank shuts at 3:30. In by 3:45, out by 4:15. Split up, then meet at Lenny's lockup to divi the proceeds. Train home and back in Colchester by 7:30. Just another day at the office, dear.

"Tickets please."

What?

Look at 'im, staring down at me like some narky screw.

Hang on. Where - ? Shit, some dips nicked me bleedin' wallet.

☙☙☙☒☙☙☙

Is this the same Lenny who we almost caught nicking ice lollies in his mis-spent youth?

It could be.

Reeling and Writhing

You might have spotted that I'm often inspired by the genius of Lewis Carroll. It seemed appropriate, therefore, to label this last section, celebrating reading and writing, by stealing one of his famous puns.

Some of these stories regale the day-to-day life of the poor, struggling writer. No doubt you imagine me wrapped in mean rags, shivering in a dimly lit garret, with no more than a few crumbs and water for sustenance. You're quite right.

Other stories simply celebrate the joy and absurdities of the English language.

I hope you enjoy them all. I very much enjoyed writing them.

(count them yourself – I've had enough)

Lost for Words

How frustrating! Desperate to write my next little story and the muse eludes me. Words just will not come. Words. Now there's an idea. Find a dictionary – a good, thick one – Collins – never fails, and let it pour its inspiration upon me. A pin; a substantial one, I think. A good, sharp hatpin - perfect. Now then, this must be done with care. I shall grasp the book in both hands and let it open randomly at a page of its choosing. Close my eyes – where's the pin? Ah – close my eyes, and with a glorious flourish I land upon...!

Lost for More Words

I must apologize for the abrupt ending to my last missive. You know how it is. You think 100 words is plenty and suddenly - no warning – the limit hits you like a brick wall. It must be frustrating for you. I will ensure it does not happen again. What am I talking about? Sorry, did you miss it? I was employing the combination of a comprehensive dictionary and a handy hatpin to furnish me with a word to inspire my next story. And the result? Let me tell you now. I'm sure it will come as no surprise – prevarication!

The Townspeople Murder Mystery

Detectives Gil Ford and Peter Burrows studied the limp body of the footman, Chester, floating in the bath. From the maid's tone, gardener, Sid Cupp, was the likely culprit, but they had the mansion house's butler, Leyton Stone, to deal with first. He revealed that the ill Chester had rushed to the loo after lunch. But it wasn't an old ham sandwich that had killed him. That was clear from the toaster and the black burn that scorched Chester's barnet.

"Don't worry," muttered Ford, "we'll pin a rap on one of them and bury you with the proper protocol, Chester."

This story has hidden within it 21 place names. Remember that this was written for a listening audience so think phonetically if you're have an itch to find them all. There are no prizes, I'm afraid, simply the glory of basking in your own success.

No Rhyme or Reason

I've never much liked poetry. It never held much joy for me, so when I'm asked to write a tale that hits a word count on the nail, I can't be arsed to tax my brain by rhyming words like rain and Spain. I just jot down my first idea, and fuelled by cigarettes and beer, I let the muse envelope me until it's time to stop for tea. It's such a simple life I lead, just writing stuff for you to read. I hope you like this latest spiel. It isn't fantasy, it's real.

Prose is best. Case rests.

Warning! Colourful Language

Do you dream of purple people eaters, live in fear of big blue meanies or worry about an invasion of little green men? Perhaps you're yellow, or you're suffering a touch of the blues. Maybe, God forbid, the black dog is at your door.

Never fear. Every cloud has a silver lining. Wash those dark thoughts away with our gold award winning recolouriser. One spray will have your neighbours green with envy. Don't get caught red-faced. Opportunities like this come once in a blue moon. One spray will have you tickled pink and ready to paint the town red again.

This was my contribution to a show about advertising commodities. Well, I'd buy some.

Writing After Midnight

When the midnight bell tolls, aspiring writers should put down their pens, close their laptops, snap shut the catches on their designer notebooks and think about grabbing a few hours of mind rejuvenating sleep.

Me? I'm scrabbling for a pencil, desperately trying to hold in the words revolving round my brain, scratching about for the tattered remnants of an exercise book or some scraps of paper discarded from the printer. And to what end? To screw them up, to throw the pencil back on the desk in despair – to hope that the morning will dawn with a little more inspiration.

It's such a shame that it rarely does.

The Seat of Learning

(SFX: A great oak door creaks open on ancient hinges)

"And here, Alfred, is where young scribes like you must sit and scratch their marks. Sit."

(SFX: Scrape of a chair being sat upon, followed by occasional clicks as it rocks on an uneven floor)

"Each sheet is carefully drawn and handed to our monks, then gathered lovingly into books."

"Books?"

"Most wonderful things, Alfred, whereby the long dead might talk to us as if still living. Thoughts and deeds put down in books might never die. Hold one, Alfred, and drink of its wonder."

"It is a weighty devil, Abbot. Do you not have something a little bit smaller?"

"Something to take about with you perhaps?"

"No, something about so thick, that will even up this wonky stool."

Making His Mark

Mark stopped drawing in the sand with his stick. "Mama, why does the old man never stop talking?"

"He is your grandfather – our storyteller. He keeps alive our tales from long ago. You see your father beside him? He listens carefully. He must learn the sagas so that he may retell them when grandfather passes. You will take his place. You must listen to their words and commit them to memory for, one day, you shall be the storyteller."

The little boy draws an ox's head in three simple lines in the sand. "I wish there was an easier way."

Piss-monunciation Syndrome

Children often come with a raft of disabilities, quirks and syndromes. This one came with enough acronyms to sink a battleship, including how to use exactly the wrong word in every conceivable situation.

Rear-Admiral Sir Double-Barrelled and his wife, knowing we had an addition to the family, thoughtfully brought a present from their travels, a stuffed elephant with a large, drooping trunk.

"And what shall you call it?" asked Lady Double-Barrelled.

"Penis."

Stunned silence.

"Penis," she shouted, assuming that, as we were over 30 we must all be stone deaf. "You know, Penis, like your friend."

"Oh, you mean Dennis!"

This Week's Latest Blockbuster

When a freak storm leaves a convention of chimney operatives abandoned on a desert island with nothing but their wits and their meagre tools to rely on, they must learn how to survive – and quickly.

Can they brush aside old enmities and make a clean sweep of things? When the dust settles, will they stack up?

And who will lead this ill-fated band? Will it be the lean and wiry Rod Driver? Does he have what it takes to reach the top and emerge victorious?

All this and more in this week's newest best seller, 'The Lord of the Flues'.

Nobody Likes Me, Everybody Hates Me, I'm Going Down the Garden to Eat Worms

I stumbled across this advert in our local newspaper this week.

FOR SALE: Author, only partly used. Has written one small book, some very short stories and some stuff he calls poetry. Comes with his own fancy pen, eleven ink cartridges and six months' supply of paper. Genuine reason for sale. Will consider exchanging for a plumbing or D-I-Y enthusiast.

I thought this was quite amusing until I spotted that the contact number was my wife's mobile.

To make matters worse, I have been following her every move for the past three days and the damn thing hasn't rung once.

I think that says it all.

Acknowledgements

If you'd like to try your hand at writing a 100-word story (or two, or more), just give it a go. It really isn't that daunting a task. All you need is a beginning, a middle and an end - preferably one that comes as a bit of surprise – a twist in the tale, you might say.

If you want to submit your lovingly crafted piece to Bill's Big Bag of Onions, it must be 100 words long (not 99, 101 or any other number you care to name). There are no other rules.

You can contact Bill Lawrence via the Bill's Big Bag of Onions Facebook page
(https://www.facebook.com/BillsBigBagOfOnions/)

Bill's Big Bag of Onions is a Guppy Production and is broadcast by Colne Radio on Tuesday evenings at 8:00pm and repeated at 10:00pm on Sundays.

It's also available on Spotify and other podcast channels

Presented by: Bill Lawrence

Producer: Adrian Coen

Voice artists: Adrian Coen and Yvonne Pini

Regular contributors include: Asia Fatima Azarah, Jake Becker, Sue Beer, Pat Blosse, Phil Boast, Angela Cairns, Adrian Coen, John Dew, Sophie Drewnogal, Simon Grinham, Ruth Hamilton, Paul Hooper, Gladys Hornet, Ian Hornet, Clare Kemsley, Bill Lawrence, Rob Lewis, Wand Lloyd, Petra McQueen, Jenny Miller, Clay Morrison, Harriet Peers, Toni Peers, Yvonne Pini, Ian Sayers and Harry Voges

(many apologies to anyone I have missed)

Printed in Great Britain
by Amazon